The Journals of Susanna Moodie

THE JOURNALS *of*

Margaret Atwood

Charles Pachter

SUSANNA MOODIE

With a memoir by Charles Pachter
and foreword by David Staines

Houghton Mifflin Company
Boston   New York   1997

Note on the Original Edition

The original edition of this work was published on October 31, 1980, in a limited edition of 120 numbered copies. It was designed by Charles Pachter and hand-printed by Manuel and Abel Bello-Sanchez.

The type was hand-set by Charles Pachter in Della Robbia, Kennerley Old Style Italic, and Goudy Old Style foundry typefaces. The original images were serigraphs, some drawn directly on screens or photo-stencils, some reworked spontaneously from lithographs, drawings, and collages.

The original edition comprised thirty-seven printed pages and required 115 separate colour runs for an edition of 120 plus two printers' proofs, resulting in 14,030 hand-pulled impressions.

FOREWORD

On the first of July, 1832, Susanna Moodie embarked from the port of Leith in Scotland for Canada with her husband and their first child. At the end of August, their ship anchored off Grosse Isle, north of Quebec City. Ten days later, the family reached their final destination, the small Lake Ontario town of Cobourg, seventy miles east of Toronto.

"In most instances, emigration is a matter of necessity, not of choice; and this is more especially true of the emigration of persons of respectable connections, or of any station or position in the world," Susanna Moodie would later write. Born near Bungay, Suffolk, on the sixth of December, 1803, and raised in a genteel family, she was already at the time of her emigration a writer of children's tales and rural sketches as well as a poet and an essayist. For a woman of her "respectable connections" and literary bent, life as a pioneer in Canada was far from easy.

For nearly eighteen months, the Moodies lived on a cleared farm near Cobourg. They then moved to a backwoods area farther north where they lived until 1840, when the family, now including five children, left the bush and settled in the town of Belleville, forty-five miles east of Cobourg.

In two autobiographical works, Susanna Moodie recalled her new environment and landscape. *Roughing It in the Bush; or, Life in Canada* (1852) details her painful pioneer life: "If these sketches should prove the means of deterring one family from sinking their property, and shipwrecking all their hopes, by going to reside in the backwoods of Canada, I shall consider myself amply repaid for revealing the secrets of the prison-house, and feel that I have not toiled and suffered in the wilderness in vain." The book's sequel, *Life in the Clearings versus the Bush* (1853), portrays the comparatively sophisticated society springing up along Lake Ontario. Mrs. Moodie's sometimes petulant and angry narrative voice in the first book gives way in the second to the voice of a resigned citizen of the new world: "Since my residence in a settled part of the country, I have enjoyed as much domestic peace and happiness as ever falls to the lot of poor humanity. Canada has become almost as dear to me as my native land; and the homesickness that constantly preyed upon me in the Backwoods, has long ago yielded to the deepest and most heartfelt interest in the rapidly increasing prosperity and greatness of the country of my adoption."

The best known of Canada's early pioneers, Susanna Moodie embodies the ambivalence of the new settler who has no choice but to confront an alien and frequently hostile terrain. She was, as Carol Shields writes, "a Crusoe baffled by her own heated imagination, the dislocated immigrant who never fully accepts or rejects her adopted country."

For Margaret Atwood, Susanna Moodie is also a dislocated and deeply divided individual: "She claims to be an ardent Canadian patriot while all the time she is standing back from the country and criticizing it as though she was a detached observer, a stranger." Moodie's personality thus reflects obsessions still haunting Canada. "We are all immigrants to this place even if we were born here: the country is too big for anyone to inhabit completely, and in the parts unknown to us we move in fear, exiles and invaders," observes Atwood. "This country is something that must be chosen – it is so easy to leave – and if we do choose it we are still choosing a violent duality."

Atwood first came upon *Roughing It in the Bush* in the family bookcase. "I did not read this book at the time. For one thing, it was not a novel, and I was not interested in books that were not novels. For another, my father told me that it was a 'classic' and that I would 'find it interesting to read some day.' I tended to shy away from books that were so described." A small excerpt from the book later appeared in her school reader. "Every author in the Grade Six reader came to us clothed in the dull grey mantle of required reading, and I forgot about Susanna Moodie and went on to other matters, such as Jane Austen."

It was during Atwood's doctoral studies at Harvard University, where she was writing her dissertation on Victorian literature, that Moodie reappeared. "I had a particularly vivid dream. I had written an opera about Susanna Moodie, and there she was, all by herself on a completely white stage, singing like Lucia di Lammermoor. I could barely read music, but I was not one to ignore portents. I rushed off to the library, where the Canadiana was kept in the bowels of the stacks beneath *Witchcraft and Demonology*, got out both *Roughing It in the Bush* and Mrs. Moodie's later work, *Life in the Clearings*, and read them at full speed."

The two books disappointed Atwood. "The prose was discursive and ornamental and the books had little shape: they were collections of disconnected anecdotes." She found "a patina of gentility that offended my young soul, as did the asides on the servant question and the lower-classness of many of the emigrants already in place." But Susanna Moodie began to haunt her: "What kept bringing me back to the subject – and to Susanna Moodie's own work – were the hints, the gaps between what was said and what hovered, just unsaid, between the lines, and the conflict between what Mrs. Moodie felt she ought to think and feel and what she actually did think and feel."

About a year and a half after her dream, Atwood began a series of poems that would become *The Journals of Susanna Moodie*, published in 1970. She did not so much recreate Moodie as create a cycle of meditations on pioneer life, on nature's relationship with its animal and human inhabitants, and on human dislocation. Although many of the poems were suggested by the Moodie books, their source was less in Moodie's words than in the words Moodie did not find.

"If the national mental illness of the United States is megalomania," Atwood concluded in 1970, "that of Canada is paranoid schizophrenia. Mrs. Moodie is divided down the middle." Atwood's Moodie is a schizoid personality. Her personal dislocation – from the old country of England which provides her perspective for seeing the new country, from the trappings of civilization, from neighbours and even family – dominates her character. She attempts to distance herself from her neighbours, even from her husband, only to discover her need for human beings as a garrison against the wilderness. She tries to explain her fascination with the Canadian landscape, yet she ends fearing her own destruction by that same landscape. She embodies what Atwood regards as the distinctly Canadian condition of living with a "violent duality."

The Journals of Susanna Moodie is divided into three entries. Journal I (1832-1840) begins with the Moodies' arrival in Canada and ends with their departure from the bush for Belleville. Journal II (1840-1871) deals with the family's years in Belleville. "At the beginning of this section," notes Atwood, "Mrs. Moodie finally accepts the reality of the country she is in, and at its end she accepts also the inescapable doubleness of her own vision." Journal III (1871-1969) takes Susanna Moodie "through an estranged old age, into death and beyond," explains Atwood. "After her death she can hear the twentieth century above her, bulldozing away her past, but she refuses to be ploughed under completely. She makes her final appearance in the present, as an old woman on a Toronto bus who reveals the city as an unexplored, threatening wilderness. Susanna Moodie has finally turned herself inside out, and has become the spirit of the land she once hated."

Susanna Moodie's haunting of Margaret Atwood did not end with the publication of *The Journals of Susanna Moodie*. In 1974 Atwood wrote a television script, *The Servant Girl*, about the convicted murderess Grace Marks, based on a story in *Life in the Clearings versus the Bush*. Later she was invited to turn her script into a play. "I wanted to open the play in the Penitentiary and close it in the Lunatic Asylum, and I had some idea of having the spirit of Susanna Moodie flown in on wires, in a black silk dress, like a cross between Peter Pan and a bat; but it was all too much for me, and I gave it up, and then forgot about it." In 1977 she published a history textbook, *Days of the Rebels 1815/1840*, which used Moodie's two books as sources.

In *Alias Grace* (1996), her ninth novel, Atwood returns to the story of Grace Marks with the intention of correcting Moodie's version: "Moodie said at the outset of her account that she was writing Grace Marks's story from memory, and as it turns out, her memory was no better than most. She got the location wrong, and the names of some of the participants, just for starters. Not only that, the actual story was much more problematic, although less neatly dramatic, than the one Moodie had told." In the novel it is Grace Marks herself who has the final word: "I have read what Mrs. Moodie wrote down about that, Sir, I said. I don't like to call anyone a liar. But Mr. MacKenzie put a misconstruction upon what I told him. . . . Mr. MacKenzie was always more fond of listening to his own voice than to someone else's."

Susanna Moodie died on the eighth of April, 1885. Through Atwood's continuing dialogue with her, she is resurrected or, more accurately, recalled. In *The Journals of Susanna Moodie*, she makes her final appearance on a bus along St. Clair Avenue, a bus route Atwood herself knows very well. "I have my ways of getting through," Atwood's Moodie affirms, and one of these ways is the art of Margaret Atwood.

For painter Charles Pachter, too, Susanna Moodie is a haunting presence from his country's past. Pachter devotes much of his work to an examination of national identity. Seizing upon commonplace objects in the Canadian landscape – the flag, the hockey player, the moose, the northern wilderness, the Queen, the Toronto streetcar – he focuses on them with such relentless and varied intensity that he compels us to reconsider these familiar signposts in our collective memory. A visual mythmaker, he seeks the reality that stands behind these objects and elevates them to the status of symbols. Through his art he remakes as strange and new our familiar iconography. "A tireless explorer of Canadian history, both local and general," according to his close friend Margaret Atwood, Pachter "has always wanted to know what is behind, before, and underneath perceived reality."

In the mid-1960s Atwood and Pachter – she, the fledgling poet, providing the text, and he, the fledgling painter, providing their visual equivalents – collaborated on five limited-edition handmade books: *The*

Circle Game (1964), *Kaleidoscopes: Baroque* (1965), *Expeditions* (1965), *Talismans for Children* (1965), and *Speeches for Doctor Frankenstein* (1966). Unprecedented in the history of Canadian art, their five books welcomed into Canada the European tradition of the *livre d'artiste*.

When he graduated in 1964 from the University of Toronto, Pachter received as a present *The Artist and the Book: 1860-1960*, a richly illustrated catalogue of an exhibition of *livres d'artistes* held in 1961 at Boston's Museum of Fine Arts. This book had an immediate and powerful effect on Pachter's artistic plans as it chronicled the turn in popularity away from the illustrated book towards the *livre d'artiste*, a unique art that brings together literary texts alongside their visual reflections. As Philip Hofer observes in his introduction to the catalogue, the word "illustrator" is no longer applicable to artists who contribute *original* graphic work to literary texts: "The painters and sculptors of wide reputation have not always been willing to illustrate, in the literal sense, the work of an author selected by the publisher. They have rather chosen, especially in recent years, to make varied and daring abstract designs, or to express new graphic ideas of their own involving complicated techniques and surface textures." Now there are, Hofer adds, "many remarkable 'modern books' that are not 'illustrated,' but 'created' or decorated, and many that are hardly books at all except in their format."

In this catalogue Pachter heard resonances of his own upbringing and the many ornate and decorated books of his childhood reading. Here, too, he discovered his own affinity with such American master graphic artists as Leonard Baskin and Ben Shahn; some of these artists – like Baskin, for example – were also printmakers. When he set out in the fall of 1964 for graduate study in lithography and design at Michigan's Cranbrook Academy of Art, he needed only Atwood's poetry to enter the realm of the *livre d'artiste*.

"The work of illustration is an act of homage to the poet," Pachter believes, and his collaborations with Atwood are labours of love, his respect for her poetry leading to his attempts to perceive and apprehend the visual image for her text. In his art Pachter seeks not to reproduce Atwood's images visually but to move inside her poems to locate an image that encapsulates some of the complexities of her text. His images complement and complete the poem, the text and the visual image functioning interdependently as a new and integrated work of art.

Pachter was, according to Atwood, distinctive among artists of his generation "in that he permitted himself a lively verbal dimension and allowed his imagination to be accessible to verbal imagery." In their collaborations, she continues, his procedure "was to immerse himself in the texture of the poetry itself for weeks, exploring its possible meanings and directions and leaving himself open to its suggestions, before starting to create his visual images. What he was able to produce was neither simple-minded illustration nor a juxtaposition of words and unrelated visual images, but an interaction between text and image that is unusual in the field."

The culmination of the Atwood-Pachter collaboration is *The Journals of Susanna Moodie*, a uniquely Canadian *livre d'artiste*. With his deeply historical sensibility and his passionate commitment to Canadian identity, Pachter recognizes in Atwood's poetic text and its central character objective correlatives for many of the themes that have been haunting his own creative imagination. Atwood's Moodie provides him with another personal encounter with his country's history and its human resources. And he, in turn, provides the poetry with a new frame, a new framework, and an evocative visual complement. Their *Journals of Susanna Moodie* is the masterwork in the long collaboration between the verbal artist and the visual artist.

David Staines
University of Ottawa, April 1997

Margaret Atwood
and Charles Pachter,
spring 1983.

AN ATWOOD/PACHTER DUET

Serendipity brought us together in the summer of 1959. We met as teenage instructors at an Ontario summer camp and became instant friends.

I taught arts and crafts. She was called "Peggy Nature" and was the custodian of a little hut where she stored insect and plant specimens and a rescued creature or two. Once, standing in a muddy field with a group of campers at her feet, she summoned me over and asked me to stroke a toad in front of the squirming kids to prove I wouldn't get warts. For the record, I did – go over and stroke the toad, and I didn't – get warts, that is. After the kids were safely tucked in bed, we would sit by the lake watching the sunset and slapping mosquitoes. I was sixteen, precocious, curious about almost everything. Peggy (the name I knew her by from the beginning) was three years older and, in my eyes, much wiser. I felt I could trust her. I asked a lot of adolescent questions. She invariably came up with thoughtful answers. E.g., Me: Do you have to suffer to make good art? She: I tried suffering, didn't like it.

If I grumbled about a teacher who didn't show the least interest in what Peggy called "the True Beauty of My Inner Soul," she'd answer back pragmatically, saying, "Never mind, some day you'll be painting God's murals in the sky and they'll all be roasting in hell."

From the first time she observed me with that quizzical gaze of hers, I relished watching her crack up at my tasteless jokes, after which she would gently scold me while offering advice on more suitable conduct. Fat chance. We took delight in each other's idiosyncrasies. Our families, hers originally Nova Scotia Anglo, mine Toronto Jewish, seemed exotic to each other.

Our friendship grew over the next two years. During her last year at the University of Toronto and my first year there, she gave me some silkscreen equipment that she had used to make posters. I took a night course in silkscreening at the Ontario College of Art and began to make posters for Hart House and for *UC Follies*. Her parents bought one of my first silkscreen prints, called *Birds in Flight*.

In 1961 Peggy gave me a copy of *Double Persephone*, her first book of hand-set poems. I was thrilled. Her words were like triggers, setting off a buzz of associations in my head and feeding a visual subconscious that I had only just begun to identify.

She left Toronto that year to pursue graduate studies at Harvard. I continued in art history at the University of Toronto and later in Paris. We corresponded, far more frequently than people do now. She often pitched my latest prints to her friends and unfailingly gave me encouragement.

I arrived at Michigan's Cranbrook Academy of Art in the fall of 1964 and began graduate studies in lithography, papermaking, and typographic design. Not long afterward, Peggy sent me a typed manuscript of her long poem *The Circle Game*. I read it once, and was overwhelmed.

My mind raced. From the first line, "The children on the lawn joined hand to hand go round and round," to the last, "I want the Circle broken," I was hooked. I felt instinctively that the medium of lithography, whose psychological nuances I was just discovering, was tailor-made for the poems. I completed printing the suite of eight poems and accompanying lithographs in three months. For the next two years I steeped myself in Atwood poetry, which she continued to send to me from Vancouver and Edmonton, where she was teaching. The more poems she sent, the more I wanted to create handmade books as handsome frameworks for them.

The Cranbrook Academy library had a fine collection of William Morris's handmade books, nineteenth-century gems from Britain's

Kelmscott Press. Other European and American private presses were also well represented. These works were tremendous inspirations. To us young artists working on the primitive antique printing presses and setting type by hand, the end result of the kiss of ink on handmade paper was a fetishistic delight. The romantic atelier atmosphere of the wooded Cranbrook campus with its 1930s Art Deco architecture was conducive to introspection. The probing literary material sent to me by Atwood fit like a glove. I decided to do my master's thesis on the methodology of illustrating poetry.

After *The Circle Game* came *Kaleidoscopes: Baroque*, a tiny book with colour woodcuts and engravings on paper that I handmade with bits of my rapidly diminishing hair, some plant material, and some chopped-up linen table napkins cadged from restaurants. *Expeditions* was next, with black-and-white lithographs and handwritten poems that I had to learn to write backwards on the lithographic plate, so they would appear right way round when printed onto paper. Then came *Talismans for Children*, with large-format colour lithographs that surrounded and permeated the printed text, blending words and images into an integrated composition for the first time. In previous folios, I had printed the text of the poetry on its own page with an accompanying image on the facing page. In *Talismans*, the text of each poem became a component part of the total visual image.

My last and most complex Cranbrook folio was *Speeches for Doctor Frankenstein*, in which I illustrated fourteen Atwood poems with combinations of linoleum cuts, silkscreens, and inked found objects pressed into the handmade paper, then folded into a quarto format. In this configuration, one large sheet of paper was folded in half twice to form a booklet with four blank pages. This required very careful printing. (If I accidentally overprinted one colour on one image inaccurately, the other three completed images on the attached quarto page became unusable.)

I completed five Atwood folios during my two years at Cranbrook. In the process I had discovered a profound harmony that resulted from the marrying of words to corresponding images. From then on, one without the other would seem bereft.

Back in Toronto in 1966, I set up a printmaking atelier in an old bicycle repair shop on Shaw Street and printed another folio of the poetry of

Printing *Speeches for Doctor Frankenstein* at Cranbrook, 1966.

prairie writer John Newlove. He and Maritimer Alden Nowlan, whose poetry I printed a couple of years later, were both referred to me by Peggy. By 1968, after moving to a new house and studio further up Shaw Street, I had acquired several fonts of antique foundry type. While I was experimenting with composing lines of text with these typefaces and printing them out on an old Vandercook proof press, Peggy sent me a typed manuscript of *The Journals of Susanna Moodie*. It was a fateful moment. I read it and was so stunned by its beauty and power that I realized everything I had done up until that moment must be a rehearsal for this.

I couldn't wait to get started. I began to work immediately on a maquette, or prototype, setting type for the poems in different styles and sizes, cutting up and collaging proofs of earlier lithographs and silkscreens, then drawing on top of them to amplify the thematic imagery of the poems. By early 1969, I had completed the typesetting and draft images for the entire suite of twenty-seven poems, with a frontispiece and two introductory images. I brought the maquette to Peggy. She enthused, suggesting I show it to Dave Godfrey and Dennis Lee, who had recently founded House of Anansi Press in Toronto (and for whom I later illustrated Dennis Lee's book of children's poems, *Wiggle to the Laundromat*). Both were eager to publish *The Journals of Susanna Moodie*, and a project proposal was submitted to the Canada Council, but it was turned down.

Peggy forged ahead and signed with Oxford University Press, which published a standard version of *The Journals of Susanna Moodie* in 1970, with some of Atwood's own unusual watercolour illustrations. With her typical optimism and resolve, she insisted that a clause be added to her contract giving me the right to produce my heftier version at any time. A signed copy of the Oxford *Susanna* soon arrived in the mail for me. Her inscription read: "To Charlie, with Regret, but Hope for the Future, Love, Peggy."

A few years later, the University of Toronto Library expressed interest in purchasing the maquette and subsequent printing rights for *The Journals of Susanna Moodie*. I wrote to Peggy in London, asking what she thought. She wrote back promptly, suggesting I hold on to them until the time was right for me to do the project my way.

Nearly a decade would pass before that right time arrived. In 1973, I bought, fixed up, and moved into an old factory just north of Queen Street at 24 Ryerson Avenue, renamed it the Artists Alliance Building, and welcomed fellow artists, writers, architects, and filmmakers as tenants. Dowdy old Queen Street West was experiencing a renaissance. I soon bought and fixed up some neighbouring warehouses, rented them out, and borrowed against their newly appraised value for further projects.

By chance, in 1979, I heard that two Spanish master printers named Abel and Manuel Bello-Sanchez were living and working in a neighbourhood loft building on Niagara Street. I called and arranged to meet them at their studio. They were experts in silkscreen, having printed editions in Europe for, among others, Salvador Dali. With the strong odour of French cigarettes and Spanish liqueurs wafting around us, we pored over the maquette, discussing various transferring and printing techniques. They cautiously agreed to sign on, provided their considerable demands were met. Soon the contract for cost of materials, edition number, printing, and payment schedules was drawn up and signed. I secured the necessary financing by borrowing against the growing equity in my loft buildings. We were ready to go.

In February 1980, I began trudging through the snow from my studio to their loft, climbing several rickety flights of stairs to the atelier where Manuel and Abel awaited me every morning. There were just the three of us. They spoke only when necessary, attending to the tasks at hand with gravity and conviction. They had set up a "drawing and thinking" table for me with crayons, grease pencils, and ink. Surrounding my table were unopened stacks of fresh paper, empty print-drying racks, newly stretched wood-framed silkscreens, and tables piled with cans of printing inks, solvents, rags, and squeegees.

Once I was satisfied with a page concept, I discussed various printing options with them. They then presented me with a blank silkscreen, leaving me alone to draw and paint on it with crayon or ink. I had to be one step ahead of them, preparing new sketches for transfer to the screens for printing while they printed previously completed drawings.

At first I worked hesitantly, but I soon went onto automatic pilot. While they dragged ink across the screens with a squeegee, printing the

Abel Bello-Sanchez
at the mixing table in
his atelier.

Manuel Bello-Sanchez
prepares a screen for
printing.

words and the images separately or together, I continued drawing directly on the silkscreens with grease crayons and tusche ink, a solution of minute grease globules suspended in water. Once the drawing was dry, they covered it and the remaining open areas of the silkscreen with a glue blockout solution and left it to dry. They then dissolved the grease-filled portions of the screen with mineral spirits so that ink could pass through the areas where I had drawn. The rhythm of watching them print layer after layer, colour over colour, washing the screens, preparing new ones for me to draw on, stacking up the finished print runs, was intoxicating.

We had an adrenaline rush each time a completed multicoloured print was added to the growing ensemble. Gradually the book took shape. Words and images began to complement one another sequentially. The poetry, set in handsome fonts of different sizes and styles, and printed in a variety of colours, seemed to jump off the page, acquiring a dimension only hinted at in the original typed manuscript.

The schedule was gruelling and exciting. We worked almost daily through spring, summer, and fall. Manuel and Abel often printed into the late hours of the night. As the seasons changed, the finished pages began to accumulate. By October 1980, they had printed over 14,000 separate impressions by hand.

We moved the completed sets of pages over to my loft-gallery on Queen Street West for sorting, proofing, and folding. Several images had been bleed-printed; that is, each blank page was first taped onto a larger undersheet of paper, then printed beyond the edges of the paper, then carefully pried free. The edges of some pages had to be hand-ripped to size (by an obliging assistant we named Pam the Ripper). All pages required hand-folding and scoring before being collated together in their proper sequence and encased in handmade calfskin suede boxes lovingly created by binder Marion Mertens.

The high that I experienced from this creative adventure may have had some influence on another project that I undertook some time later. In the early summer of 1981, I began working on a series of paintings of the Canadian flag. It was seven months since we had completed the poem "Death of a Young Son by Drowning" from *The Journals of Susanna Moodie*, in which the last line is "I planted him in this country like a flag."

The Journals of Susanna Moodie was launched in October 1980 at a party in the loft-gallery where we had laboured to assemble each book. I think it is fair to say that it set a new standard for the handmade *livre d'artiste* in Canada. As a poetic evocation of the travails experienced by a nineteenth-century genteel English immigrant in her new Canadian homeland, it is also a landmark literary work.

In 1984, to mark the bicentennial of the arrival of Loyalist immigrants from the new United States in what is now Ontario, *The Journals of Susanna Moodie* was first exhibited at the Art Gallery of Ontario. The exhibition later travelled throughout the province, and to Halifax and Calgary, and was featured in the exhibition *Books by Artists/Livres d'artistes* at the National Gallery of Canada in Ottawa. Paul Hassoun, French cultural attaché in Toronto, became interested in the Atwood/Pachter collaboration in 1991 and produced an elegant French translation of the poems.

Sara Borins was just a year old in 1969 when I completed the first maquette for *The Journals of Susanna Moodie*. In 1995, while working at Macfarlane Walter & Ross, Sara called to ask me if I realized that it was *Susanna*'s "twenty-fifth anniversary" and suggested I consider doing a facsimile version of the original limited edition. I was dubious. I had turned down earlier offers. But she persisted, promising that it would be done to my satisfaction. And the result is this accessible, artist-supervised version now available to a much wider readership than could be reached through the original "élite" edition of 120 copies.

Marriage of the creative efforts of two fellow voyagers, *The Journals of Susanna Moodie* is nothing if not my homage to the writer, poet, and friend whose genius has been a sustained source of inspiration for my imagination. And so I dedicate this:

To Peggy, to whom I will always remain profoundly grateful.

Charles Pachter
Toronto, April 1997

I take this picture of myself
and with my sewing scissors
cut out the face.

Now it is more accurate;

Where my eyes were
every-
thing appears

I take this picture of myself
and with my sewing scissors
cut out the face.

Now it is more accurate;

Where my eyes were
-every-
thing appears

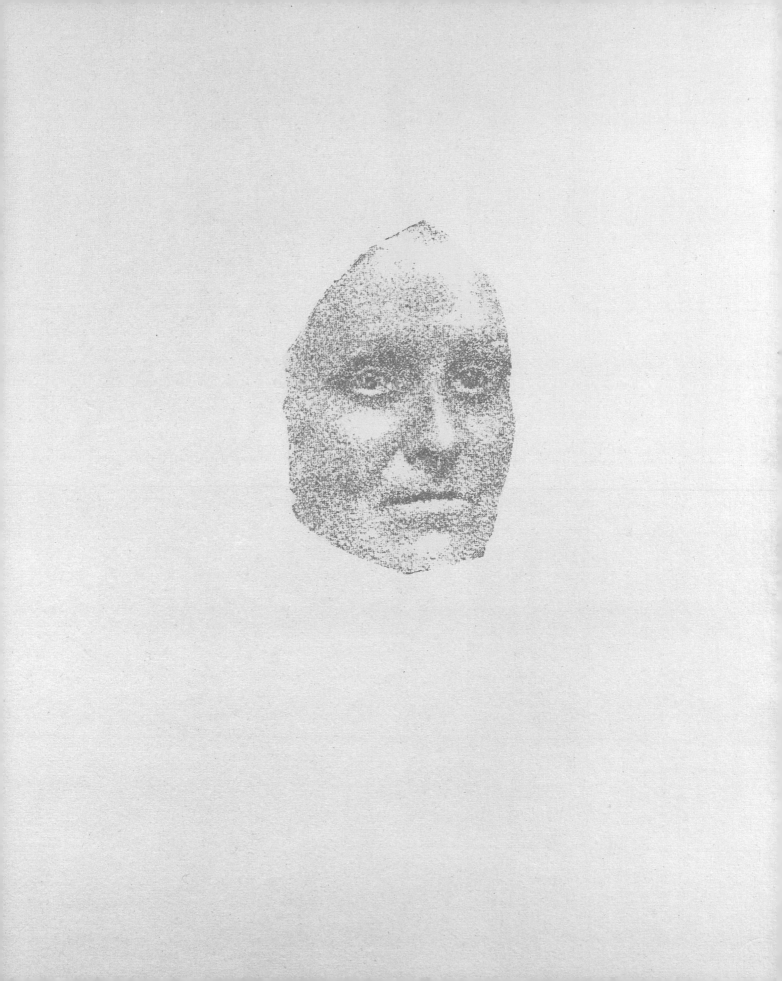

Margar...

THE JOU...
SUSANNA...

Charle...

Atwood

RNALS OF

MOODIE

Pachter

JOURNAL ONE

1832-1840

DISEMBARKING IN QUEBEC

Is it my clothes, my way of walking,
the things I carry in my hand
- a book, a bag with knitting -
the incongruous pink of my shawl

this space cannot hear

or is it my own lack
of conviction which makes
these vistas of desolation,
long hills, the swamps, the barren sand, the glare
of sun on the bone-white
driftlogs, omens of winter,
the moon alien in day-
time a thin refusal

The others leap, shout

        Freedom!

The moving water will not show me
my reflection.

The rocks ignore.

I am a word
in a foreign language.

FURTHER ARRIVALS

After we had crossed the long illness
that was the ocean, we sailed up-river

On the first island
the immigrants threw off their clothes
and danced like sandflies

We left behind one by one
the cities rotting with cholera,
one by one our civilized
distinctions

and entered a large darkness.

It was our own
ignorance we entered.

I have not come out yet

My brain gropes nervous
tentacles in the night, sends out
fears hairy as bears,
demands lamps; or waiting

for my shadowy husband, hears
malice in the trees' whispers.

I need wolf's eyes to see
the truth.

I refuse to look in a mirror.

Whether the wilderness is
real or not
depends on who lives there.

FIRST NEIGHBOURS

The people I live among, unforgivingly
previous to me, grudging
the way I breathe their
property, the air,
speaking a twisted dialect to my differently-
shaped ears

though I tried to adapt

(the girl in a red tattered
petticoat, who jeered at me for my burned bread

Go back where you came from

I tightened my lips; knew that England
was now unreachable, had sunk down into the sea
without ever teaching me about washtubs)

got used to being
a minor invalid, expected to make
inept remarks,
futile and spastic gestures

(asked the Indian
about the squat thing on a stick
drying by the fire: Is that a toad?
Annoyed, he said No no,
deer liver, very good)

Finally I grew a chapped tarpaulin
skin; I negotiated the drizzle
of strange meaning, set it
down to just the latitude:
something to be endured
but not surprised by.

Inaccurate. The forest can still trick me:
one afternoon while I was drawing
birds, a malignant face
flickered over my shoulder;
the branches quivered.

Resolve: to be both tentative and hard to startle
(though clumsiness and
fright are inevitable)

in this area where my damaged
knowing of the language means
prediction is forever impossible

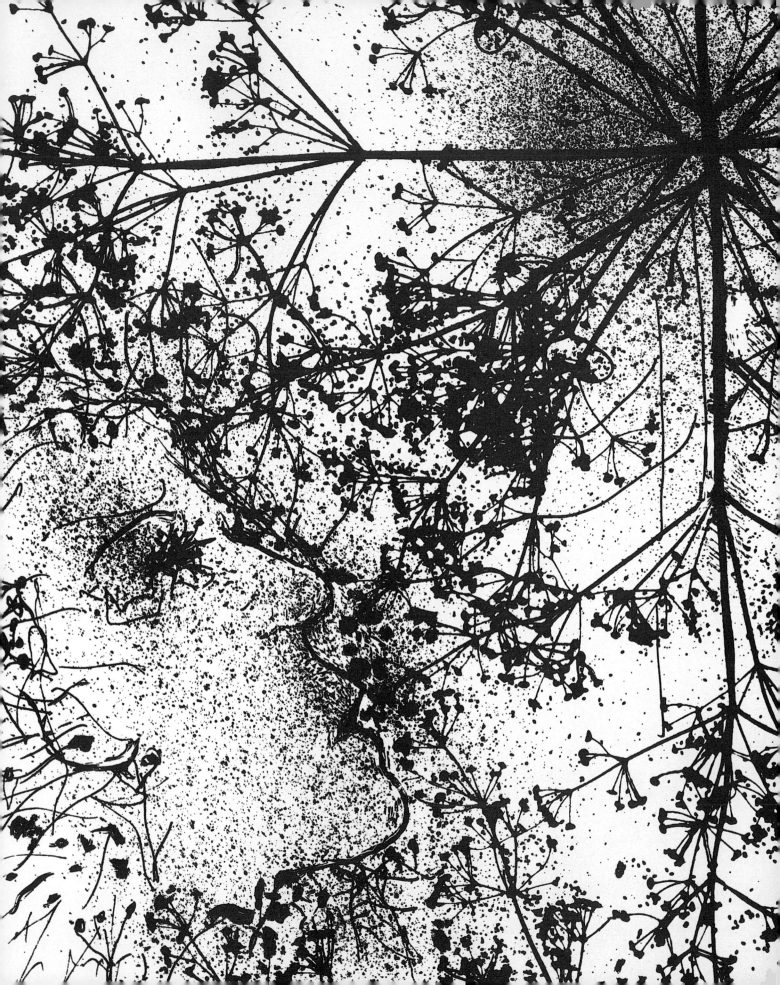

THE PLANTERS

They move between the jagged edge
of the forest and the jagged river
on a stumpy patch of cleared land

my husband, a neighbour, another man
weeding the few rows
of string beans and dusty potatoes.

They bend, straighten; the sun
lights up their faces and hands, candles
flickering in the wind against the

unbright earth. I see them; I know
none of them believe they are here.
They deny the ground they stand on,

pretend this dirt is the future.
And they are right. If they let go
of that illusion solid to them as a shovel,

open their eyes even for a moment
to these trees, to this particular sun
they would be surrounded, stormed, broken

in upon by branches, roots, tendrils, the dark
side of light
as I am.

THE WEREMAN

My husband walks in the frosted field
an X, a concept
defined against a blank;
he swerves, enters the forest
and is blotted out.

Unheld by my sight
what does he change into
what other shape
blends with the under-
growth, wavers across the pools
is camouflaged from the listening
swamp animals

At noon he will
return; or it may be
only my idea of him
I will find returning
with him hiding behind it.

He may change me also
with the fox eye, the owl
eye, the eightfold
eye of the spider

I can't think
what he will see
when he opens the door

PATHS AND THINGSCAPE

Those who went ahead
of us in the forest
bent the early trees
so that they grew to signals:

the trail was not
among the trees but
the trees

and there are some who have dreams
of birds flying in the shapes
of letters; the sky's
codes,
        and dream also
the significance of numbers (count
petals of certain flowers)

> In the morning I advance
> through the doorway: the sun
> on the bark, the inter-
> twisted branches, here
> a blue movement in the leaves, dispersed
> calls/ no trails; rocks
> and grey tufts of moss
>
> The petals of the fire-
> weed fall where they fall
>
> I am watched like an invader
> who knows hostility but
> not where
>
> The day shrinks back from me

When will be
that union and each
thing (bits
of surface broken by my foot
step) will without moving move
around me
into its place

THE TWO FIRES

One, the summer fire
outside: the trees melting, returning
to their first red elements
on all sides, cutting me off
from escape or the saving
lake

I sat in the house, raised up
between that shapeless raging
and my sleeping children
a charm: concentrate on
form, geometry, the human
architecture of the house, square
closed doors, proved roofbeams,
the logic of windows

(the children could not be wakened:
in their calm dreaming
the trees were straight and still
had branches and were green)

The other, the winter
fire inside: the protective roof
shrivelling overhead, the rafters
incandescent, all those corners
and straight lines flaming, the carefully-
made structure
prisoning us in a cage of blazing
bars
            the children
were awake and crying;
I wrapped them, carried them
outside into the snow.
Then I tried to rescue
what was left of their scorched dream
about the house: blankets,
warm clothes, the singed furniture
of safety cast away with them
in a white chaos

Two fires in-
formed me,

(each refuge fails
us; each danger
becomes a haven)

left charred marks
now around which I
try to grow

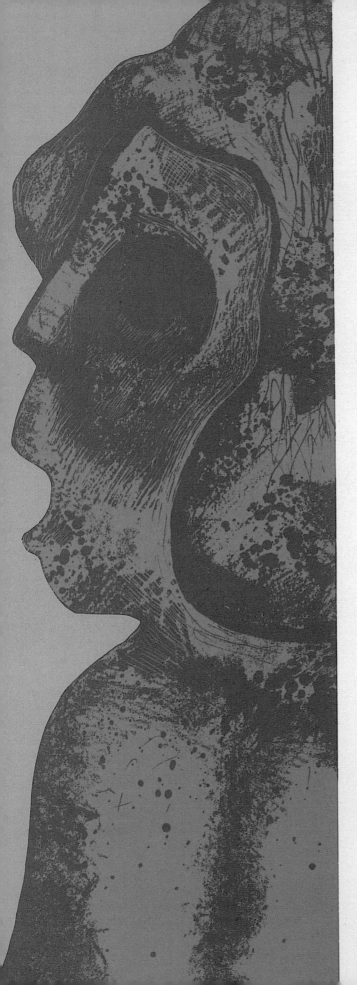

LOOKING IN A MIRROR

It was as if I woke
after a sleep of seven years

to find stiff lace, religious
black rotted
off by earth and the strong waters

and instead my skin thickened
with bark and the white hairs of roots

My heirloom face I brought
with me a crushed eggshell
among other debris:
the china plate shattered
on the forest road, the shawl
from India decayed, pieces of letters

and the sun here had stained
me its barbarous colour

Hands grown stiff, the fingers
brittle as twigs
eyes bewildered after
seven years, and almost
blind/buds, which can see
only the wind

the mouth cracking
open like a rock in fire
trying to say

What is this

(you find only
the shape you already are
but what
if you have forgotten that
or discover you
have never known)

LOOKING IN A MIRROR

It was as if I woke
after a sleep of seven years

to find stiff lace, religious
black rotted
off by earth and the strong waters

and instead my skin thickened
with bark and the white hairs of roots

My heirloom face I brought
with me a crushed eggshell
among other debris:
the china plate shattered
on the forest road, the shawl
from India decayed, pieces of letters

and the sun here had stained
me its barbarous colour

Hands grown stiff, the fingers
brittle as twigs
eyes bewildered after
seven years, and almost
blind/buds, which can see
only the wind

the mouth cracking
open like a rock in fire
trying to say

What is this

(you find only
the shape you already are
but what
if you have forgotten that
or discover you
have never known)

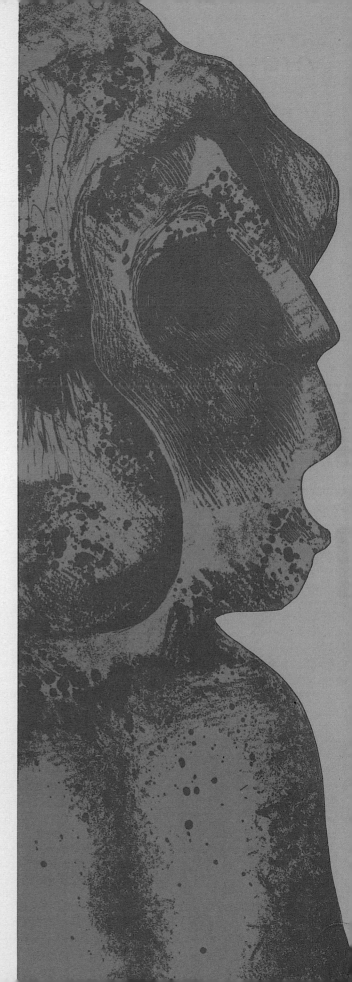

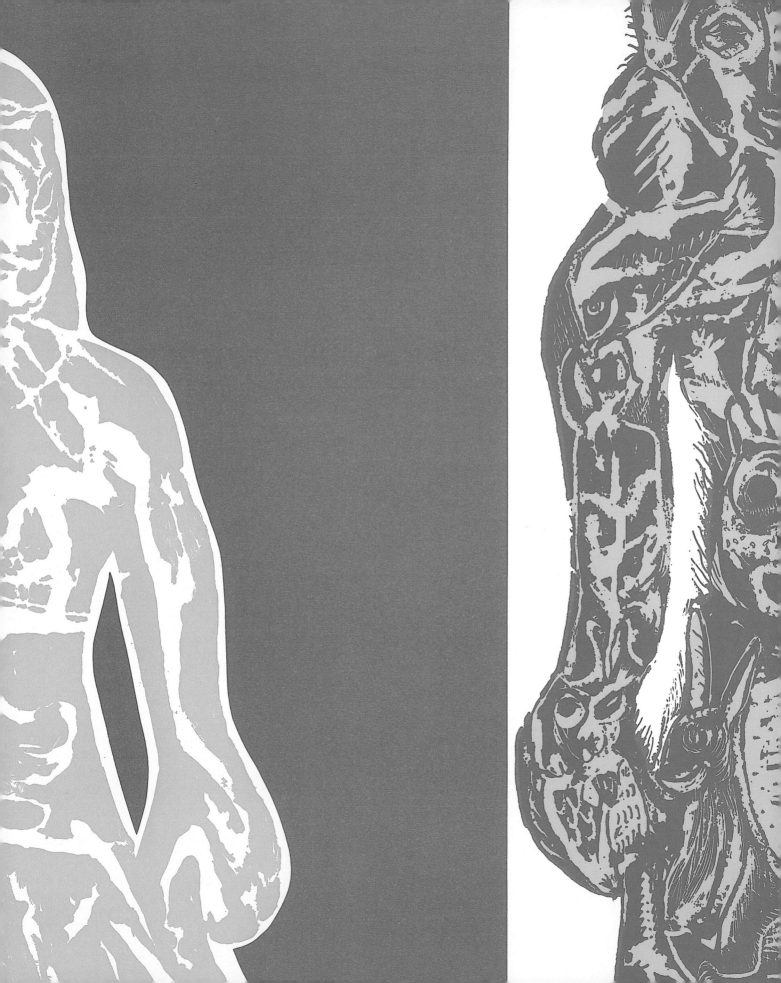

DEPARTURE FROM THE BUSH

I, who had been erased
by fire, was crept in
upon by green
                        (how
lucid a season)

                In time the animals
arrived to inhabit me,

first one
  by one, stealthily
(their habitual traces
burnt); then
having marked new boundaries
returning, more
confident, year
by year, two
by two

but restless: I was not ready
altogether to be moved into

They could tell I was
too heavy: I might
capsize;

I was frightened
by their eyes (green or
amber) glowing out from inside me

I was not completed; at night
I could not see without lanterns.

He wrote, We are leaving. I said
I have no clothes
left I can wear

The snow came. The sleigh was a relief;
its track lengthened behind,
pushing me towards the city

and rounding the first hill, I was
(instantaneous)
unlived in: they had gone.

There was something they almost taught me
I came away not having learned.

JOURNAL TWO
1840-1871

DEATH OF A YOUNG SON BY DROWNING

He, who navigated with success
the dangerous river of his own birth
once more set forth

on a voyage of discovery
into the land I floated on
but could not touch to claim.

His feet slid on the bank,
the currents took him;
he swirled with ice and trees in the swollen water

and plunged into distant regions,
his head a bathysphere;
through his eyes' thin glass bubbles

he looked out, reckless adventurer
on a landscape stranger than Uranus
we have all been to and some remember.

There was an accident; the air locked,
he was hung in the river like a heart.
They retrieved the swamped body,

cairn of my plans and future charts,
with poles and hooks
from among the nudging logs.

It was spring, the sun kept shining, the new gras
leapt to solidity;
my hands glistened with details.

After the long trip I was tired of waves.
My foot hit rock. The dreamed sails
collapsed, ragged.

I planted him in this country
like a flag.

THE IMMIGRANTS

They are allowed to inherit
the sidewalks involved as palmlines, bricks
exhausted and soft, the deep
lawnsmells, orchards whorled
to the land's contours, the inflected weather

only to be told they are too poor
to keep it up, or someone
has noticed and wants to kill them; or the towns
pass laws which declare them obsolete.

I see them coming
up from the hold smelling of vomit,
infested, emaciated, their skins grey
with travel; as they step on shore

the old countries recede, become
perfect, thumbnail castles preserved
like gallstones in a glass bottle, the
towns dwindle upon the hillsides
in a light paperweight-clear.

They carry their carpetbags and trunks
with clothes, dishes, the family pictures;
they think they will make an order
like the old one, sow miniature orchards,
carve children and flocks out of wood

but always they are too poor, the sky
is flat, the green fruit shrivels
in the prairie sun, wood is for burning;
and if they go back, the towns

in time have crumbled, their tongues
stumble among awkward teeth, their ears
are filled with the sound of breaking glass.
I wish I could forget them
and so forget myself:

my mind is a wide pink map
across which move year after year
arrows and dotted lines, further and further,
people in railway cars

their heads stuck out of the windows
at stations, drinking milk or singing,
their features hidden with beards or shawls
day and night riding across an ocean of unknown
land to an unknown land.

THE

They
the s
exha
lawn
to th

only
to ke
has
pass

I see
up f
infes
with

DREAM 1: THE BUSH GARDEN

I stood once more in that garden
sold, deserted and
gone to seed

In the dream I could
see down through the earth, could see
the potatoes curled
like pale grubs in the soil
the radishes thrusting down
their fleshy snouts, the beets
pulsing like slow amphibian hearts

Around my feet
the strawberries were surging, huge
and shining

When I bent
to pick, my hands
came away red and wet

In the dream I said
I should have known
anything planted here
would come up blood

1837 WAR IN RETROSPECT

One of the
things I found out by being
there, and after:

that history (that list
of ballooning wishes, flukes,
bent times, plunges and mistakes
clutched like parachutes)

is rolling itself up in your head
at one end and unrolling at the other

that this war will soon be among
those tiny ancestral figures
flickering dull white through the back of your skull,
confused, anxious, not sure any more
what they are doing there

appearing from time to time
with idiot faces and hands clusters
of bananas, holding flags,
holding guns, advancing through the trees
brown line green scribble

or crouching within a rough grey
crayon diagram of a fort,
shooting at each other, the smoke and red fire
made actual through a child's fingers.

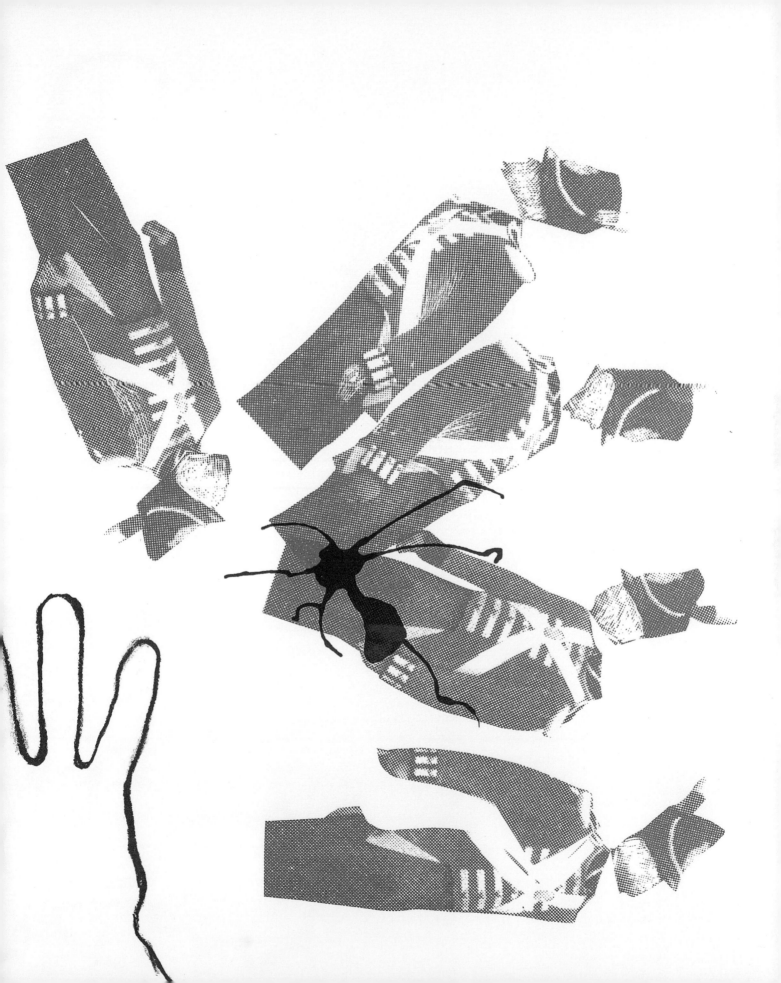

DREAM 2: BRIAN THE STILL-HUNTER

The man I saw in the forest
used to come to our house
every morning, never said anything;
I learned from the neighbours later
he once tried to cut his throat.

I found him at the end of the path
sitting on a fallen tree
cleaning his gun.

There was no wind;
around us the leaves rustled.

He said to me:
I kill because I have to

but every time I aim, I feel
my skin grow fur
my head heavy with antlers
and during the stretched instant
the bullet glides on its thread of speed
my soul runs innocent as hooves.

Is God just to his creatures?

I die more often than many.

He looked up and I saw
the white scar made by the hunting knife
around his neck.

When I woke
I remembered: he has been gone
twenty years and not heard from.

CHARIVARI

"They capped their heads with feathers, masked
their faces, wore their clothes backwards, howled
with torches through the midnight winter

and dragged the black man from his house
to the jolting music of broken
instruments, pretending to each other

it was a joke, until
they killed him. I don't know
what happened to the white bride."

The American lady, adding she
thought it was a disgraceful piece
of business, finished her tea.

(Note: Never pretend this isn't
part of the soil too, teadrinkers, and inadvertent
victims and murderers, when we come this way

again in other forms, take care
to look behind, within
where the skeleton face beneath

the face puts on its feather mask, the arm
within the arm lifts up the spear:
Resist those cracked

drumbeats. Stop this. Become human.)

DREAM 3: NIGHT BEAR WHICH FRIGHTENED CATTLE

Horns crowding toward us
a stampede of bellowing, one
night the surface of my mind keeps
only as anecdote

We laughed, safe with lanterns
at the kitchen door

though beneath stories

where forgotten birds
tremble through memory, ripples across water
and a moon hovers in the lake
orange and prehistoric

I lean with my feet grown intangible
because I am not there

watching the bear I didn't see condense
itself among the trees, an outline
tenuous as an echo

but it is real, heavier
than real   I know
even by daylight here
in this visible kitchen

it absorbs all terror

it moves toward the lighted cabin
below us on the slope
where my family gathers

a mute vibration passing
between my ears

THE DEATHS OF THE OTHER CHILDREN

The body dies

little by little

the body buries itself

joins itself
to the loosened mind, to the black-
berries and thistles, running in a
thorny wind
over the shallow
foundations of our former houses,
dim hollows now in the sandy soil

Did I spend all those years
building up this edifice
my composite
                self, this crumbling hovel?

My arms, my eyes, my grieving
words, my disintegrated children

Everywhere I walk, along
the overgrowing paths, my skirt
tugged at by the spreading briers

they catch at my heels with their fingers

THE DOUBLE VOICE

Two voices
took turns using my eyes:

One had manners,
painted in watercolours,
used hushed tones when speaking
of mountains or Niagara Falls,
composed uplifting verse
and expended sentiment upon the poor.

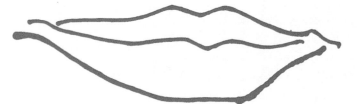

The other voice
had other knowledge:
that men sweat
always and drink often,
that pigs are pigs
but must be eaten
anyway, that unborn babies
fester like wounds in the body,
that there is nothing to be done
about mosquitoes;

One saw through my
bleared and gradually
bleaching eyes, red leaves,
the rituals of seasons and rivers

The other found a dead dog
jubilant with maggots
half-buried among the sweet peas.

JOURNAL THREE

1871-1970

LATER IN BELLEVILLE: CAREER

Once by a bitter candle
of oil and braided
rags, I wrote
verses about love and sleighbells

which I exchanged for potatoes;

in the summers I painted butterflies
on a species of white fungus
which were bought by the tourists, glass-
cased for English parlours

and my children (miraculous)
wore shoes.

Now every day
I sit on a stuffed sofa
in my own fringed parlour, have
uncracked plates (from which I eat
at intervals)
and a china teaset.

There is no use for art.

DAGUERROTYPE TAKEN IN OLD AGE

I know I change
have changed

but whose is this vapid face
pitted and vast, rotund
suspended in empty paper
as though in a telescope

the granular moon

I rise from my chair
pulling against gravity
I turn away
and go out into the garden

I revolve among the vegetables,
my head ponderous
reflecting the sun
in shadows from the pocked ravines
cut in my cheeks, my eye-
sockets 2 craters

along the paths
I orbit
the apple trees
white white spinning
stars around me

I am being
eaten away by light

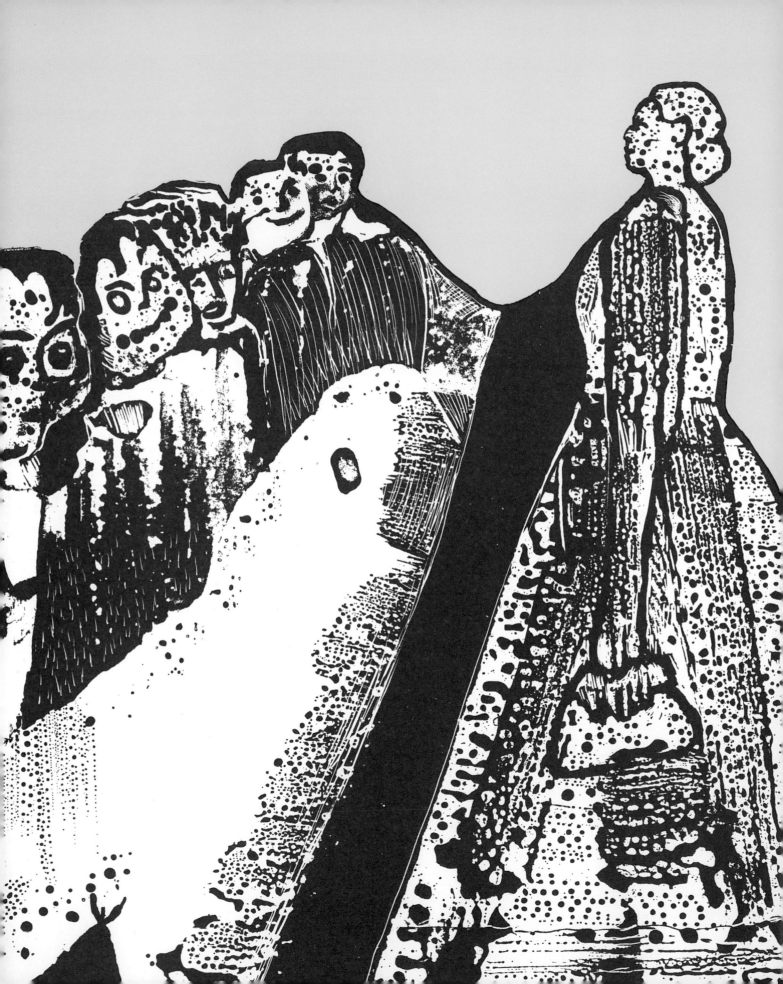

WISH: METAMORPHOSIS TO HERALDIC EMBLEM

I balance myself carefully
inside my shrinking body
which is nevertheless
deceptive as a cat's fur:

when I am dipped in the earth
I will be much smaller.

On my skin the wrinkles branch
out, overlapping like hair or feathers.

In this parlour my grandchildren
uneasy on sunday chairs
with my deafness, my cameo brooch
my puckered mind
scurrying in its old burrows

little guess how
                maybe

I will prowl and slink
in crystal darkness
among the stalactite roots, with new
formed plumage
               uncorroded
                    gold and

fiery green, my fingers
curving and scaled, my

opal
    no
  eyes glowing

VISIT TO TORONTO, WITH COMPANIONS

The streets are new, the harbour
is new also;
the lunatic asylum is yellow.

On the first floor there were
women sitting, sewing;
they looked at us sadly, gently,
answered questions.

On the second floor there were
women crouching, thrashing,
tearing off their clothes, screaming;
to us they paid little attention.

On the third floor
I went through a glass-panelled
door into a different kind of room.
It was a hill, with boulders, trees, no hous
I sat down and smoothed my gloves.

The landscape was saying something
but I couldn't hear. One of the rocks
sighed and rolled over.

Above me, at eye level
three faces appeared in an oblong space.

They wanted me to go out
to where there were streets and
the Toronto harbour

I shook my head. There were no clouds, the flowers
deep red and feathered, shot from among
the dry stones,

                    the air
was about to tell me
all kinds of answers

SOLIPSISM WHILE DYING

the skeleton produces flesh

enemy
opposing, then taken
for granted, earth harvested, us
up, walked over

the ears produce sounds

what I heard I
created. (voices
determining, repeating
histories, worn customs

the mouth produces words

I said I created
myself, and these
frames, commas, calendars
that enclose me

the hands produce objects

the world touched
into existence: was
this cup, this village here
before my fingers

the eyes produce light

the sky
leaps at me: let there be
the sun-
set

Or so I thought, lying in the bed
being regretted

added: What will they do now
that I, that all
depending on me disappears?
Where will be Belleville?

Kingston?

(the fields
I held between.   the lake
boats

t o r o N T O

THOUGHTS FROM UNDERGROUND

When I first reached this country
I hated it
and I hated it more each year:

in summer the light a
violent blur, the heat
thick as a swamp,
the green things fiercely
shoving themselves upwards, the
eyelids bitten by insects

in winter our teeth were brittle
with cold. We fed on squirrels.
At night the house cracked.
In the mornings, we thawed
the bad bread over the stove.

Then we were made successful
and I felt I ought to love
this country.
                    I said I loved it
and my mind saw double.

I began to forget myself
in the middle
of sentences. Events
were split apart

I fought. I constructed
desperate paragraphs of praise, everyone
ought to love it because

and set them up at intervals

        due to natural resources, native industry, superior
        penitentiaries
        we will all be rich and powerful

flat as highway billboards

        who can doubt it, look how
        fast Belleville is growing

(though it is still no place for an english gentleman)

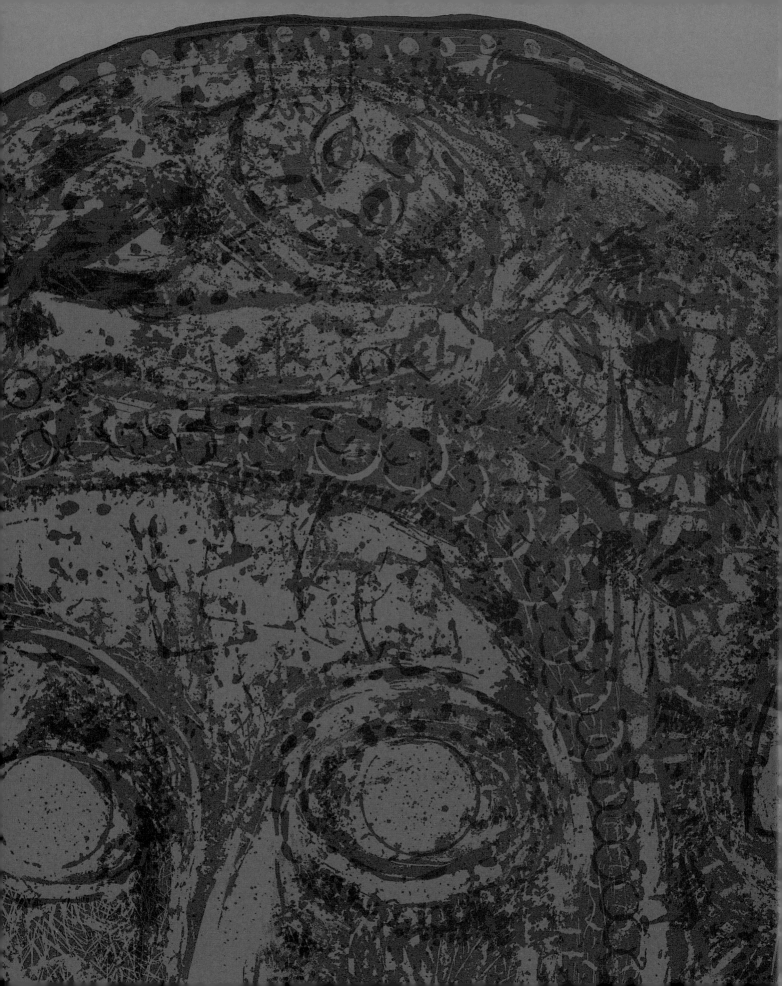

ALTERNATE THOUGHTS FROM UNDERGROUND

Down. Shovelled. Can hear
faintly laughter, footsteps;
the shrill of glass and steel

the invaders of those for whom
shelter was wood,
fire was terror and sacred

the inheritors, the raisers
of glib superstructures.

My heart silted by decades
of older thoughts, yet prays

O topple this glass pride, fireless
rivetted babylon, prays
through subsoil
to my wooden fossil God.

But they prevail. Extinct. I feel
scorn but also pity: what
the bones of the giant reptiles

done under by the thing
(may call it
climate) outside the circle
they drew by their closed senses
of what was right

felt when scuttled
across, nested in by the velvet immoral
uncalloused and armourless mammals.

RESURRECTION

I see now I see
now I cannot see

earth is a blizzard in my eyes

I hear now

          the rustle of the snow

the angels listening above me

          thistles bright with sleet
          gathering

waiting for the time
to reach me
up to the pillared
sun, the final city

          or living towers

unrisen yet
whose dormant stones lie folding
their holy fire around me

(but the land shifts with frost
and those who have become the stone
voices of the land
shift also and say

god is not
the voice in the whirlwind

god is the whirlwind

at the last
judgment we will all be trees